FOREWORD

WELCOME TO THIS GUIDE ALL ABOUT LICHFIELD CATHEDRAL - AN ANCIENT CATHEDRAL FULL OF LIFE AND WONDER. IN THESE PAGES YOU WILL FIND OUT ABOUT THE RICH PAST, THE TURMOIL IT HAS ENDURED, THE CRAFTMANSHIP THAT MAKES IT UNIQUE AND THE PEOPLE, PAST AND PRESENT, THAT HAVE SHAPED THE CATHEDRAL, THE CITY OF LICHFIELD AND THE REGION.

As you explore these pages may you discover new things and encounter something beyond mere facts and figures - the faith that is the bedrock of Lichfield Cathedral.

ABOUT LICHFIELD CATHEDRAL

Lichfield Cathedral and its Close is one of the most exquisite settings in England. The views of the Cathedral from the south, across the two pools, provide an unrivalled vista. It is a visual glory, and it is justly prized.

Its collection of glass, artefacts, sculpture, furnishings and its historic library and Anglo-Saxon treasures render it uniquely interesting, architecturally significant (Grade 1 listed) and of outstanding historical importance.

It provides a glorious focus for worship and reaches out to communities across the Diocese (the third largest in England), offering support to a wide range of missional and charitable activities.

The Cathedral provides space for worship, community, and cultural events. This follows a tradition that has been handed down through the generations since the first Cathedral was founded in 700 on the burial site of St Chad, making it among the earliest centres of Christian worship in the UK.

CONTENTS

Site plan	P04
History & timeline	P06
1. West Front, Exterior & The Close	P08
2. The Nave	P12
3. The Crossing	P14
4. The North Transept	P15
5. The Pedilavium & Chapter House	P16
6. The Quire, Presbytery & High Altar	P20
7. North & South Quire Aisles	P22
8. Lady Chapel and Shrine of St Chad	P24
9. St Chad's Head Chapel	P28
10. St Michael's Chapel and South Transept	P30
The Cathedral today	P32
Get Involved	P33
Calendar of events	P34
Glossary of terms	P35

SITE PLAN

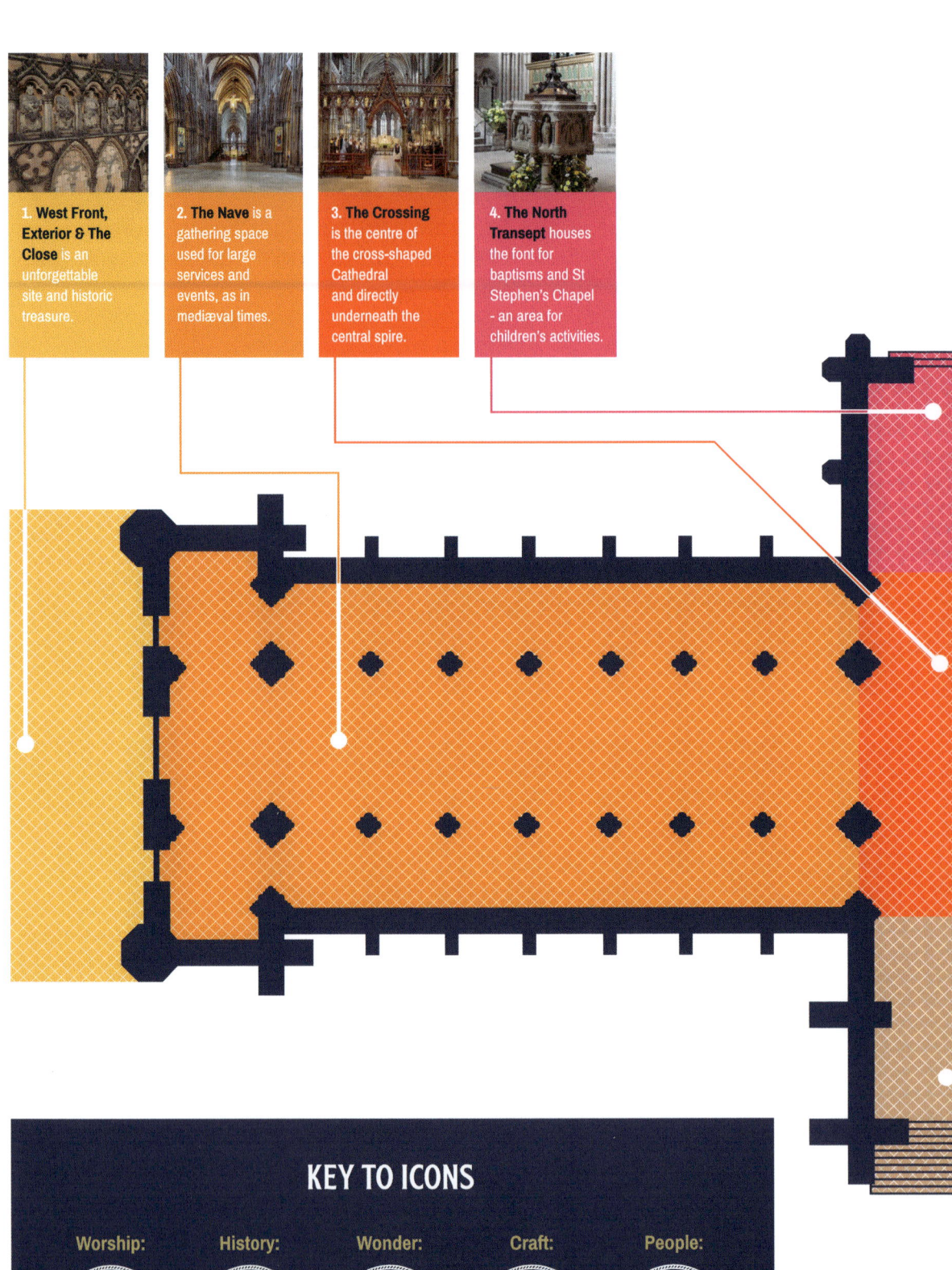

1. West Front, Exterior & The Close is an unforgettable site and historic treasure.

2. The Nave is a gathering space used for large services and events, as in mediæval times.

3. The Crossing is the centre of the cross-shaped Cathedral and directly underneath the central spire.

4. The North Transept houses the font for baptisms and St Stephen's Chapel - an area for children's activities.

KEY TO ICONS

Worship: History: Wonder: Craft: People:

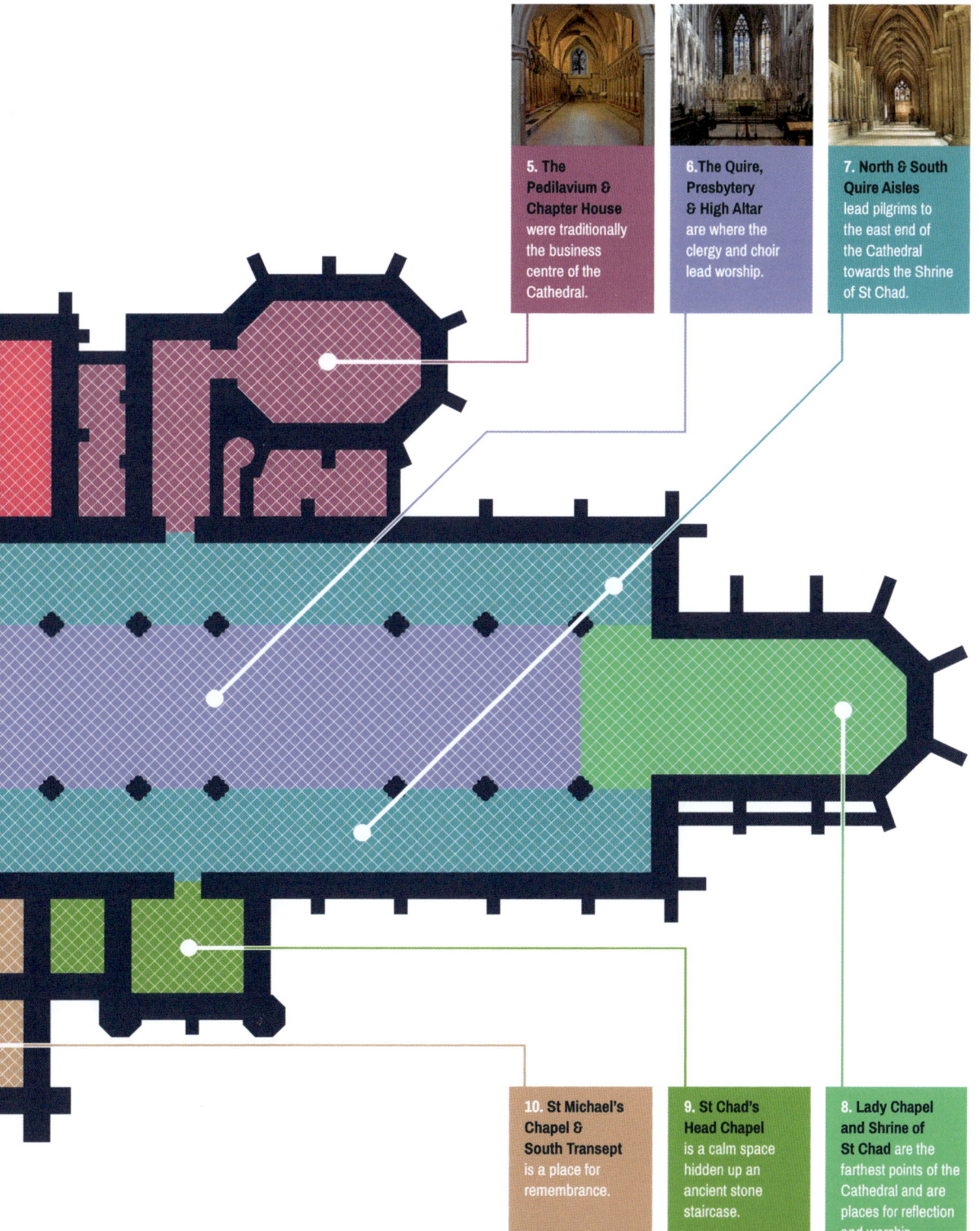

HISTORY

ANGLO SAXON CATHEDRAL
Lichfield is a city today because of the Cathedral, first built in 700AD by Bishop Hedda to house the relics of St Chad, the inspiring Bishop of Mercia who died in 672. The Anglo-Saxon cathedral remained until the beginning of the twelfth century when it was demolished and rebuilt by the Normans.

DAMAGED CATHEDRAL
Like other religious foundations, Lichfield Cathedral suffered damage in the sixteenth century. Statues were defaced and destroyed, walls and paintings were whitewashed, and the Shrine of St Chad was dismantled.

RESTORED CATHEDRAL
Extensive damage to the main fabric and to the interior meant that in 1660 only the Chapter House was usable. Bishop Hacket spent his own money restoring the Cathedral, although some of the damaged carvings have been left unrestored as a reminder of the past.

The whole interior had been whitewashed during the turmoil of the Civil War, and the mediæval glass had been destroyed during the sixteenth and seventeenth centuries. It was into these austere surroundings that, in 1803, Dean Proby introduced coloured Flemish glass from the abbey at Herkenrode.

TODAY'S CATHEDRAL
The major preoccupation of the twentieth and twenty-first centuries has been the preservation of the building, which is ongoing and expensive. Restorative work to the Herkenrode glass and a major overhaul of the stonework has been completed. The Shrine of St Chad was reinstated in 2022.

MEDIÆVAL CATHEDRAL
Most of the present-day Cathedral dates from this rebuilding, including St Chad's Head Chapel and the Chapter House. In the first years of the fourteenth century Bishop de Langton began work on the construction of the Lady Chapel. He also paid for a new shrine for St Chad.

SIEGED CATHEDRAL
During the Civil War, in the seventeenth century, the Cathedral suffered enormous damage. It was occupied at the beginning of hostilities and endured three sieges, during the course of which the central spire fell into the church after being hit by a cannonball.

VICTORIAN CATHEDRAL
The most far-reaching refurbishment was undertaken in the nineteenth century, when Dean Howard and the Chapter decided that they would try to bring back the feeling of a mediæval English cathedral. By the beginning of the twentieth century the interior of the Cathedral was much as it is now.

DID YOU KNOW?

Ladies of the Vale
The three spires of the Cathedral are known locally as 'The Ladies of the Vale', and they can be seen from all directions. When the spires were completed there had already been a cathedral on the site for six hundred years.

TIMELINE

669	Chad becomes Bishop
672	Chad dies of plague
700	First Cathedral dedicated
1085-1140	Second Cathedral built
1195-1208	Presbytery & Quire erected
1225	St Chad's Head Chapel completed
1249	Chapter House completed
1280-1289	Nave built
1323	West Front completed
1320-1330	Lady Chapel built
1490	Library built
1538	Destruction of St Chad's Shrine
1643-1660	3 sieges during Civil War
1660-1669	Cathedral restored
1802-1804	Herkenrode glass installed
1856-1908	Cathedral restorations
1956-1966	Roof restored
2000	Organ rebuilt and enlarged with almost 1000 additional pipes in the Nave
2003-2004	Discovery of the Lichfield Angel
2009-2015	Herkenrode glass restored
2016-2018	Chapter House & Library repairs
2021-2022	Flying buttress repairs
2022	Shrine of St Chad reinstated

1. WEST FRONT, EXTERIOR & THE CLOSE

IN THE SIXTEENTH CENTURY THE ANTIQUARIAN JOHN LELAND CALLED THE WEST FRONT 'THE GLORY OF THE CHURCH' AND HE PRAISED THE ROWS OF STATUES WHICH STILL COVER THE WEST FRONT.

IT IS ASSUMED THAT IN MEDIÆVAL TIMES THE FIGURES WERE GILDED – THE SIGHT OF GILDED STATUES AGAINST THE RED STONE MUST HAVE ASTONISHED PILGRIMS AS THEY APPROACHED THE CATHEDRAL.

WHAT TO LOOK FOR:

Of the 113 figures only five, high on the north tower, are mediæval; the others were placed here in the 1880s to replace damaged or missing statues.

Look out for:
- Anglo-Saxon and post-Norman Conquest Kings
- Old Testament Prophets
- Saints & Martyrs
- Archangels
- Bishops

GREAT WEST DOORS

Around the great west doors, which still have some of their thirteenth-century ironwork and weigh one and a half tonnes, are several carvings of particular significance: St Chad sits immediately above the door; on the column is a nineteenth-century carving of the Virgin and Child; and within the porch is a 14th century carving of Christ in Majesty.

WEST FRONT APEX

The nineteenth-century statue at the apex of the west front is of Christ, as it was in the Middle Ages. After the Restoration of the monarchy in 1660, King Charles II was put in this position, only to be removed by the Victorians. His statue was subsequently moved to the south side of the building.

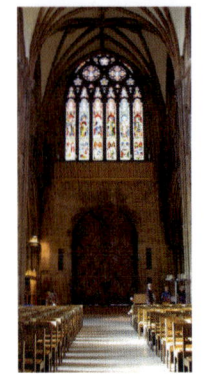

Opposite: Lichfield Cathedral West Front
Left (top): North west doorway featuring the female saints
Left (bottom left): Great West Doors from inside the Cathedral
Left (middle right): Statue of St Mary and the Christ Child by the Great West Doors
Left (bottom right): Weather vane on the south spire

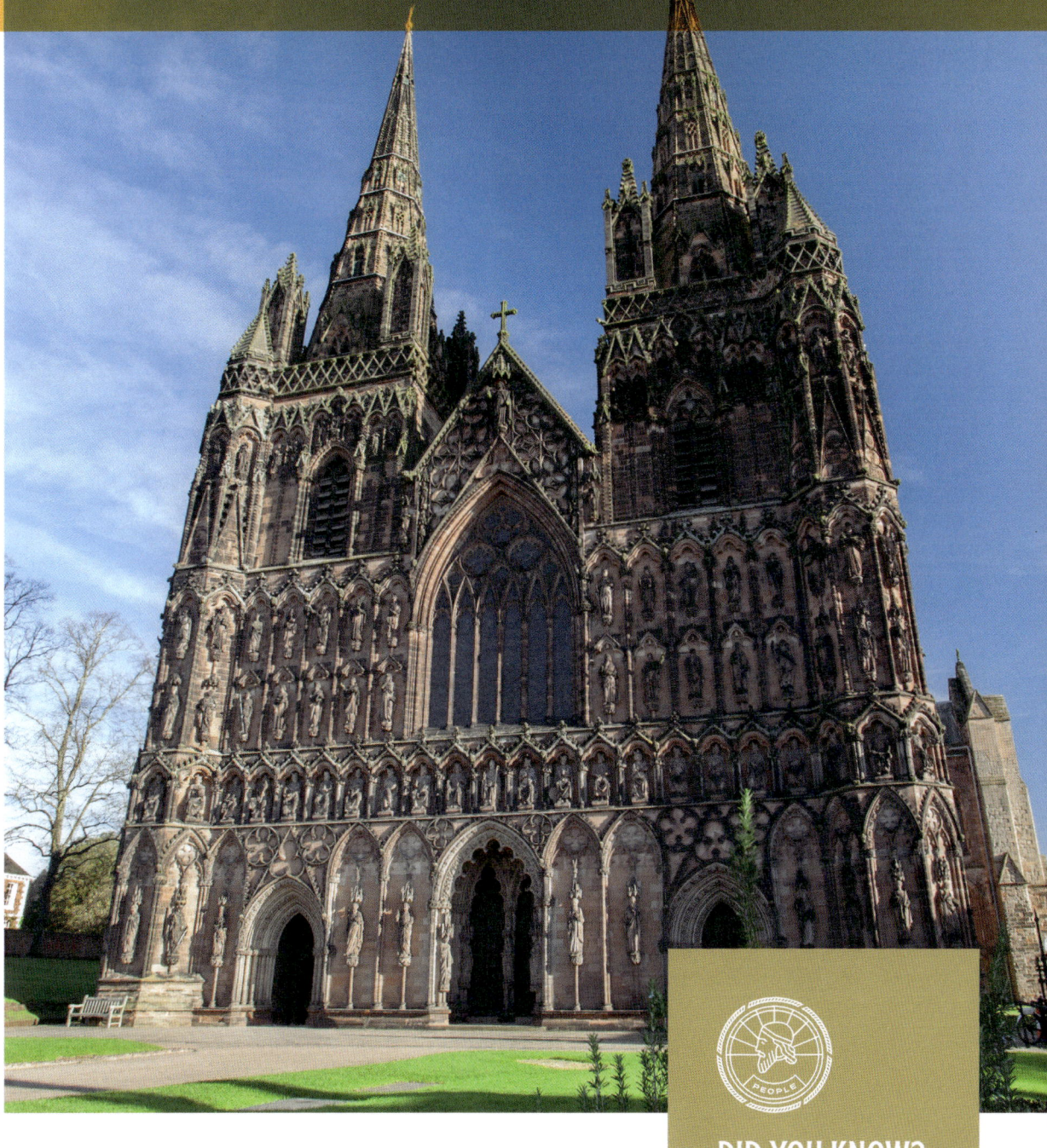

THE TWO TOWERS
Of the two towers, the north provided space for the singing school and the south, which in the past was called the Jesus Bell Tower, still houses the peal of ten bells. The bells were removed during the Civil War and were replaced by Bishop Hacket. They were recast after the Second World War.

SINGING HOLES
Between the two towers, within the thickness of the wall, is a passage, which cannot be seen from inside the Cathedral. A number of narrow openings on the outside, partially hidden by the statues, allowed choristers to sing out to worshippers waiting below.

STATUE RESTORATION
The recent need to repair damaged stonework has provided the opportunity for modern masons to produce new carvings. There has been extensive work at high level to the Lady Chapel, Chapter House, Quire Aisles, and Flying Buttresses with new gargoyles added to the east end.

And he was afraid, and said, 'How awesome is this place! This is none other than the house of God, and this is the gate of heaven.' (Gen 28.17)

DID YOU KNOW?
The West Front is famous for its statues depicting people who have shaped the life of Lichfield and the nation, but as you walk through the North-West doors you will see a beautifully carved tribute to female saints, lesser-known heroines of the Christian faith.

THE CLOSE

The Cathedral Close and its buildings share a rich history. Originally the Close was surrounded by large fortifications including a perimeter wall (remnants of which can still be seen), a moat and two impressive gates.

Whilst the exterior of many of the buildings have changed over the centuries, many of the houses are built upon the original mediæval foundations.

FACING THE CATHEDRAL

To the west are some large, detached houses of mediæval origin. Although these have been altered extensively over the centuries much of their original, mediæval foundations exist beneath their Victorian facades.

HIDDEN COURTYARDS

In the 14th century, land was given to create two closes with a common hall in the centre for the Vicars Choral, whose role was, and still is, to sing the services. The upper courtyard is Vicars Close, consisting of timber framed houses built in the 14th and 15th centuries. The lower courtyard is now the herb garden at the back of the Erasmus Darwin Museum. The half-timbered houses in the courtyards are still occupied, but no longer exclusively by the Lay Vicars.

WHAT TO LOOK FOR:

- Remains of the gatehouses are still visible at both entrances to The Close
- Vicars Close was built in the 1470s to house the Vicars Choral whose role was to sing services
- Many of the original mediæval houses were given new frontages in later centuries
- The former Bishop's Palace is now part of Lichfield Cathedral School

Opposite: The Bishop's Palace, now part of Lichfield Cathedral School
Below: Vicars Close
Opposite (bottom left): Statue of St Chad by Peter Walker
Opposite (bottom right): Statue of Charles II moved to the South Transept steps

DID YOU KNOW?

Newton's College was built along the west entrance to The Close in the nineteenth century for the accommodation of the widows and orphans of the clergy.

BISHOP'S PALACE
Until the twentieth century, the bishops of Lichfield had a palace on the north side of the Cathedral. The mediæval palace was large enough to house visiting monarchs such as King Richard II, but it suffered extensive damage in the Civil War, and a new, smaller Palace was built in 1687. This eventually became part of the Cathedral School.

THE DEANERY
Next to the Bishop's Place is The Deanery, a charming building, built between 1705 and 1707.

COLLEGE HALL
On the south side of the main Close the chantry priests, whose task it was to say Masses for the souls of the dead, were gathered together in the building known as New College. A theological college for the training of priests was built in 1857 on the site. The building is now called College Hall even though the college closed in 1972.

2. THE NAVE

THE NAVE WAS ALWAYS TRADITIONALLY THE PUBLIC SPACE OF THE CATHEDRAL. ORIGINALLY THERE WOULD NOT HAVE BEEN SEATS, SO THAT IT COULD BE USED FOR PUBLIC GATHERINGS, AND WORSHIP.

LARGE NUMBERS OF PEOPLE NOW GATHER HERE FOR SERVICES AND EVENTS. IT IS ALSO USED FOR CONCERTS, THEATRICAL PERFORMANCES, CONFERENCES, AND DINNERS.

WHAT TO LOOK FOR:

- In Mediæval times the interior walls were coloured, mostly red and green, and small traces of mediæval paint can still be seen in places
- Carved stone faces look into the Nave from the walls, each representing worshippers and pilgrims of the Mediæval times

Opposite: Vaulting in the Nave Aisles
Below: The Nave featuring the Icon of Jesus Crucified
Opposite (middle left): Jesus Christ carved stone face
Opposite (middle right): Writing of the icon The Annunciation
Opposite (bottom): Stained glass featured in North Nave Aisle

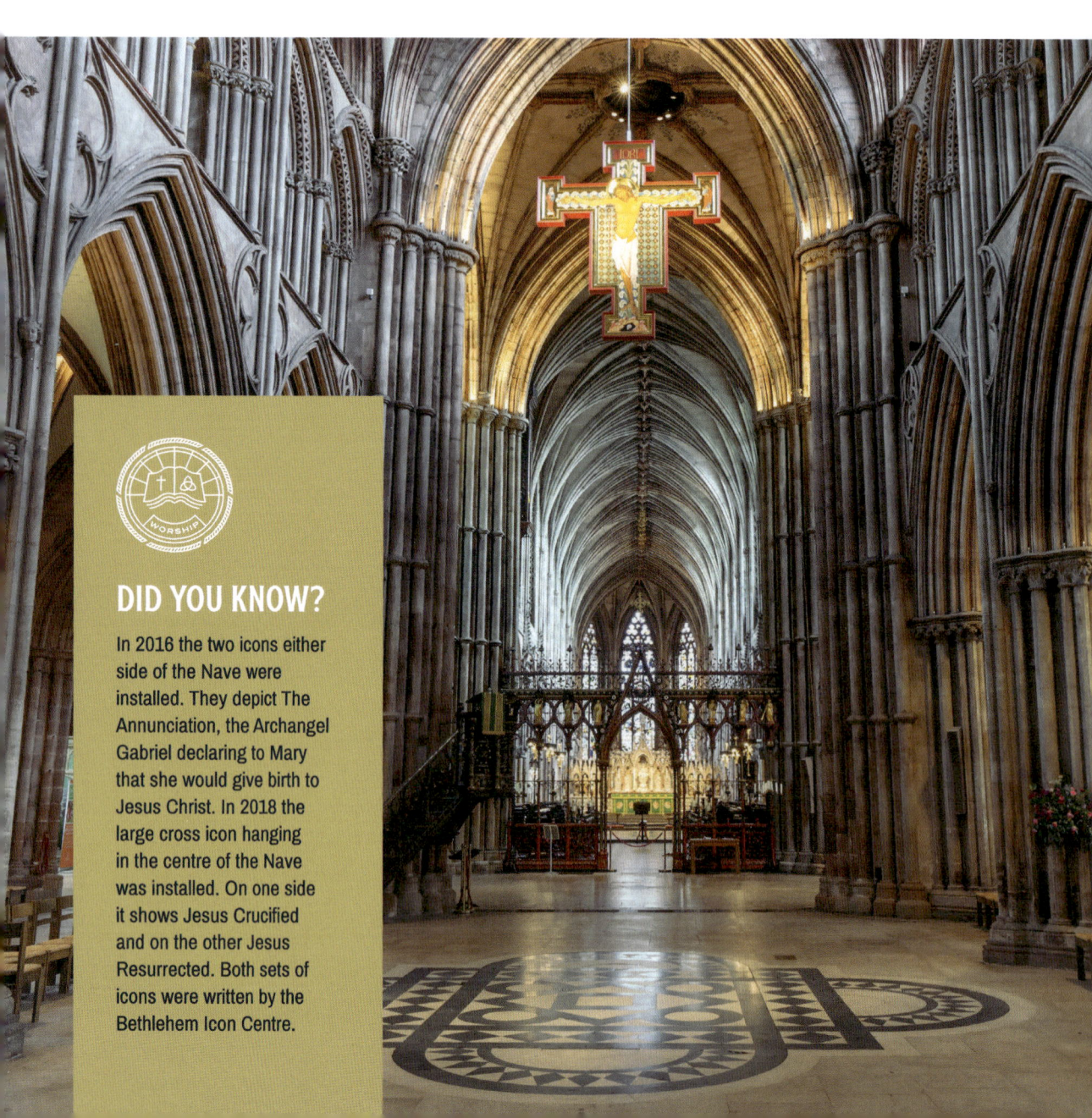

DID YOU KNOW?

In 2016 the two icons either side of the Nave were installed. They depict The Annunciation, the Archangel Gabriel declaring to Mary that she would give birth to Jesus Christ. In 2018 the large cross icon hanging in the centre of the Nave was installed. On one side it shows Jesus Crucified and on the other Jesus Resurrected. Both sets of icons were written by the Bethlehem Icon Centre.

'For when two or three are gathered in my name, I am there among them.'
(Matthew 18.20)

SLOPING WALLS
The Nave retains some thirteenth-century features, including its tall, elegant columns and clerestory windows. The cutting-edge design was eventually found to be flawed; the weight of the stone vaulting forced the walls outwards. In fact, at their centre, the arcade pillars are 14 inches out from the vertical to the top. Architect James Wyatt replaced most of the original stone vaulting with a wood and plaster copy at the end of the eighteenth century to stop the ceiling collapsing in on itself.

SEATING
In mediæval times worshippers would have stood, but the elderly and infirm could use the stone bench around the wall. From this we get the expression – 'The weakest go to the wall'.

To mark the Millennium, a group of 181 needleworkers created cushions for the stone bench. Each cushion has the heraldry/symbol of parishes within the Diocese and across all 117 cushions there are over 540 churches represented, showing just how vast the Diocese of Lichfield is.

CARVED STONE FACES
The carving at higher levels is mediæval, but during the Victorian restoration it was necessary to replace the lower carvings and to restore parts of the blind arcading. The darker stone, and crisper lines of the later work make it easy to distinguish. The faces represent the worshippers of the Middle Ages, including the face of Christ, wearing the Crown of Thorns, sitting among the congregation.

 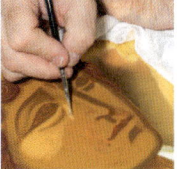

NAVE ALTAR
The Nave altar was replaced in 2003 and a retractable platform installed in 2004. During the excavations in 2003, a piece of Anglo-Saxon sculpture known as The Lichfield Angel (now located in the Chapter House) was found. This area may have been the site of the original shrine of St Chad in the eighth century.

3. THE CROSSING

THE CROSSING IS LITERALLY THE CRUX OF THE CATHEDRAL'S CROSS-SHAPED BUILDING, DIRECTLY UNDERNEATH THE CENTRAL SPIRE.

DID YOU KNOW?

During the military occupations of Lichfield Cathedral by both sides in the Civil War there was extensive damage and vandalism. Not only did the Central Spire collapse causing severe damage, but also monuments, stained glass and carvings were destroyed. Some records suggest that parliamentary soldiers may have used the Nave to stable their horses.

'Suffering produces endurance, and endurance produces character, and character produces hope, and hope does not disappoint us, because God's love has been poured into our hearts.' (Romans 5.3-5)

PULPIT
Designed by George Gilbert Scott and made by Skidmore (of Coventry) from wrought iron, copper, brass, enamel, and marble. The bronze group in the centre depicts Peter preaching on the day of Pentecost. Two staircases counterbalance the pulpit, which is supported by a small pillar.

SKIDMORE SCREEN
In 1857 the architect Smirke removed the stone screen that would have separated the congregation from the clergy and choir. Later that year George Gilbert Scott designed a new screen, which was installed in 1861. The screen, like many features in the Cathedral, was inspired by Chad's vision of angels and features angels playing instruments that are mentioned in Psalm 150.

CENTRAL SPIRE
During the Civil War Lichfield Cathedral came under siege three times and was occupied for much of the war. The Cathedral was ransacked, the Central Tower was struck by cannon balls and later collapsed into the building. A stained-glass window in the South Quire Aisle depicts the efforts of Bishop Hacket in the 1660s to restore the ransacked Cathedral.

THE ORGAN
From the Crossing there is a good view of the organ (above the North Quire stalls) and its 5038 pipes. The current organ was installed in 1884 by William Hill & Son and then moved to its current position in 1908. In 2000 Harrison & Harrison rebuilt the organ and added just under 1000 pipes into the triforium (the section above the North Nave Aisle) to allow for better sound in the Nave.

WHAT TO LOOK FOR:

Throughout Lichfield Cathedral you will find angels in carvings, stained glass, and metal work. Angels are special to the Cathedral in that they recall the story (told in the Venerable Bede's Ecclesiastical History) of Chad's vision of angels coming to take him to glory, just a week before his death.

On this page:
View of the organ from the Quire

4. THE NORTH TRANSEPT

THE NORTH TRANSEPT IS HOME TO SEVERAL IMPORTANT MONUMENTS, BEAUTIFUL STAINED GLASS, A SMALL CHAPEL AND A PLACE WHERE BAPTISMS ARE HELD.

WHAT TO LOOK FOR:

- There are some interesting details carved into the sides of the font that children enjoy finding, including animals from various angles
- At the foot of the monument to John Lonsdale in St Stephen's Chapel there is a particularly fierce looking dragon - he would conduct 'the examination and criticism of the monthly sermons of Deacons'

On this page: Hands of the Bishop Ryder statue

'Go therefore and make disciples of all nations, baptizing them in the name of the Father and of the Son and of the Holy Spirit, ... and remember, I am with you always, to the end of the age.' (Matthew 28.19-20)

DID YOU KNOW?

The large window in the North Transept was restored in 1893 in the style of the original 13th century window, alongside repairs to the stonework. The glass, supplied by Clayton and Bell, depicts the Tree of Jesse, the father of King David, from whose line came Jesus Christ.

THE FONT
The Font, previously housed in the Nave but moved in 1982, was given to Lichfield Cathedral by the Hon. Mrs Howard (widow of Dean Howard) in 1860. The side scenes relate to Baptism: Noah's Ark, the Parting of the Red Sea, the Baptism of Jesus, and the Resurrection of Jesus. Figures in the niches portray St Mary, St Peter, St Chad and St Helen.

DEAN HEYWOOD'S MONUMENT
One of the most energetic and generous Deans of Lichfield, Heywood was commemorated with a double monument, but the upper section was destroyed in the Civil War. Above was Heywood in his robes, and below the effigy of his cadaver – this and monuments like it were often used as a preaching point to illustrate how no matter who we are, we all die and our bodies decay.

BISHOP RYDER
Bishop Ryder was Bishop of Lichfield from 1824, and was highly regarded for his evangelistic work, having opened 22 new churches in his short 8-year posting, amongst other things. This sculpture by Chantrey, commemorates him and his important work.

ST STEPHEN'S CHAPEL
This small chapel, which was made smaller in 2000 to provide some essential storage space, is now used as an area for children and families to be creative, read books and learn about Bible stories. It is also used for regular children's activities during school holidays.

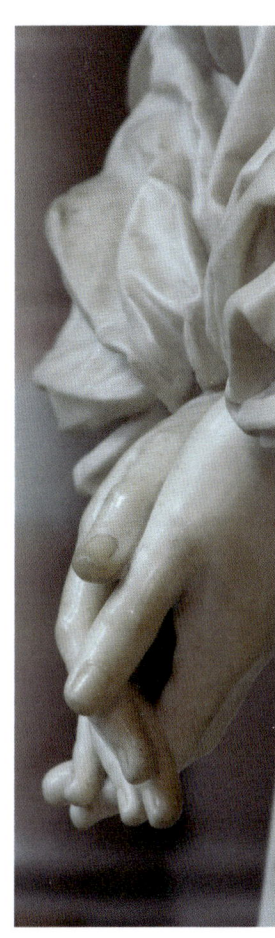

5. THE PEDILAVIUM & CHAPTER HOUSE

THE PEDILAVIUM IS THE LINK BETWEEN THE NORTH QUIRE AISLE AND THE CHAPTER HOUSE. THE WHOLE AREA WAS PROBABLY USED AS A WAITING ROOM FOR THOSE COMING TO DO BUSINESS IN THE CHAPTER HOUSE. THIS IS WHERE THE CLERGY AND CHOIR GATHER AT THE BEGINNING AND END OF SERVICES EVERY DAY.

PEDILAVIUM
Pilgrims in mediæval times and modern times may have had their feet washed here in traditional fashion, which is why the space is sometimes referred to as the pedilavium, coming from the latin 'pedes' (feet) and 'lavare' (wash).

BISHOP WOODS
Near the entrance to the Chapter House there is a bust by the world-renowned sculptor, Jacob Epstein, of Bishop Woods, who was Bishop of Lichfield during the Second World War.

CHAPTER HOUSE
The Chapter House was built in the 1240s. Set into the walls are stone seats; in the Mediæval times representatives of the two Chapters of Coventry and Lichfield gathered here to elect a bishop for their joint diocese. The double mitre over the bishop's own seat signals this. A special gathering of the College of Canons still meets in the Chapter House on St Chad's Day every year.

WHAT TO LOOK FOR:

There are some interesting stone carvings, some of which are mediæval, to look out for in the Chapter House:

- Christ above the doorway
- A cat with a mouse
- A boy-bishop wearing an overlarge mitre
- A green man and a green woman (a typical green man carving shows a face appearing from foliage)

Opposite: 13th Century vaulting in the Chapter House
Below (top left): Bishop Woods by Jacob Epstein
Below (bottom left): Mediæval wall painting
Below (right): View down the Pedilavium

'Worship the Lord in holy splendour... all the earth.'
(Ps 96.9)

TWO PATRON SAINTS

On the wall above the entrance inside the Chapter House is one of three mediæval wall paintings in the Cathedral. It shows the Assumption of the Blessed Virgin Mary, who is one of the Cathedral's two patron saints. The other, St Chad, appears in the stained glass, which was made in the studios of Kempe and Burlisson & Grylls. The windows show various scenes from the life of St Chad, including his education by St Aidan on Lindisfarne and the visit by angels to foretell his death.

DID YOU KNOW?

The Library has c. 7000 books, of which Frances Seymour, Duchess of Somerset gave a large number of books from her husband, William Seymour's library at the same time as returning the St Chad Gospels.

THE LICHFIELD ANGEL

The Lichfield Angel is a late eighth-century stone carving of the Archangel Gabriel in the role of messenger, which was found in the Nave during excavations in 2003.

It probably formed part of an Annunciation scene and was paired with a carving of the Blessed Virgin Mary.

The carving appears to have been part of a stone chest – perhaps containing the relics of St Chad – all part of a stone shrine that was built to replace the original wooden shrine described by the Venerable Bede in 731.

Above: The 13th Century Library
Left: The 8th Century Lichfield Angel
Opposite (top left): Carved bird detail
Opposite (top right): Carved stone tilted head
Opposite (middle): Illustrated page from the 8th Century St Chad Gospels
Opposite (bottom): Detail from one of the map books, part of the Library Collection

ST CHAD GOSPELS

The St Chad Gospels (also known as the 'Lichfield Gospels') date from around the same time as the Lichfield Angel and contains the gospels of St Matthew, St Mark and some verses of St Luke's Gospel; the rest of it was presumably lost during its turbulent history. At some point it was in Wales, where pages of it were used to record land transactions and, in the margins, it has some of the earliest known examples of written Welsh. During the seventeenth century it was handed over to the Duchess of Somerset for safekeeping during the Civil War.

The volume is still used occasionally as a Gospel Book on solemn occasions. Bishops, Deans and Canons take their Declaration of Fidelity to the Cathedral Foundation on it, which must mean that it is one of the oldest books in Britain still used for its original purpose.

THE LIBRARY

The central column in the Chapter House rises to an upper storey, which houses the Library. When it was first built it may have housed all the Cathedral's treasures, including its books. In the fifteenth century two deans, who wished to encourage scholars to come to Lichfield as canons, built a new library on the north side of the Cathedral; this library was demolished in the eighteenth century.

The Cathedral's rich collection of mediæval manuscripts and early printed books was lost through destruction and dispersal during the Civil War. In the 1670s, the room above the Chapter House became a new library to house a bequest from the Duchess of Somerset of her late husband's library. The library's collection has grown through further gifts and bequests. It now contains a number of illuminated manuscripts, including a copy of Chaucer's Canterbury Tales dating from 1420, and an interesting collection of Bibles, such as Wycliffe's translation of the New Testament (1410) and a King Henry VIII The Great Bible (1539). Tours of the Library take place a number of times each year, and tickets may be purchased in advance; special arrangements can also be made for small-group visits.

6. THE QUIRE, PRESBYTERY & HIGH ALTAR

THIS PART OF THE CATHEDRAL HAS BEEN REBUILT SEVERAL TIMES OVER THE CENTURIES. THE SITE OF ANGLO-SAXON WORSHIP AND PART OF THE NORMAN CATHEDRAL, IT WAS REBUILT IN THE LATE TWELFTH CENTURY AND MODIFIED WHEN THE LADY CHAPEL WAS ADDED IN THE FOURTEENTH CENTURY. IT WAS RADICALLY ALTERED IN THE EIGHTEENTH CENTURY, AND FINALLY THE VICTORIANS REANIMATED IT AS THE HEART OF THE CHURCH.

QUIRE
The Quire is used regularly for daily services, notably for the singing of Evensong. The choir is made up of the gentlemen of the choir (the Lay Vicars Choral), choral scholars, a boys' choir and a girls' choir. The Chamber Choir supplement the Choral Foundation for services and concerts. Visiting choirs and musicians also contribute to the musical life of the Cathedral.

CATHEDRA
The Bishop's Seat or Cathedra is located here and this is where the name 'Cathedral' comes from. It is a symbol of the Bishop's authority and is located here because the Cathedral is the Mother Church of the Diocese of Lichfield.

DID YOU KNOW?

The music-making in the quire is complemented by the stone angels on the corbels who, like those in the rest of the quire and elsewhere in the Cathedral, play and sing to the glory of God.

TILES

Victorian roundels on the presbytery floor illustrate stories from the life of St Chad: his consecration as bishop, the Archbishop lifting Chad onto a horse, and the bringing of his bones into the Cathedral by Bishop Hedda. The story of Precentor Higgins who was instrumental in returning the Cathedral to Anglican worship, is also shown.

HIGH ALTAR

Sir George Gilbert Scott designed the new high altar using materials from the Diocese: alabaster from Fauld near Tutbury, grey and red marble and Blue John from Derbyshire and Staffordshire, and tiles from Stoke-on-Trent. He also tried to reuse materials or reinstate the mediæval layout and design. The sedilia (the ceremonial seats on each side of the altar) are made from elaborately carved Bath limestone from the mediæval Cathedral.

'And suddenly there was with the angel a multitude of the heavenly host, praising God and saying, 'Glory to God in the highest heaven, and on earth peace among those whom he favours!' (Luke 2.13-14)

WHAT TO LOOK FOR:

- The evidence of restoration can be seen in the leaf carving on the columns, where the later, more elaborate forms replace the earlier simpler ones

- On one of the columns on the north side, almost opposite the Bishop's Seat (Cathedra), the face of a man looking out from the leaves is said to be that of William Ramsey, the King's Master Mason, appointed in 1337

Opposite: View of the High Altar from the Quire
Above (left): An angel from the Skidmore Screen
Above (right): The cross at the top of the High Altar reredos

7. NORTH & SOUTH QUIRE AISLES

THE AISLES ON EITHER SIDE OF THE QUIRE LEAD TO THE PRESBYTERY AND HIGH ALTAR, AND FURTHER EASTWARDS TO THE STUNNING LADY CHAPEL. THERE ARE MEMORIALS TO PROMINENT FIGURES IN THE CATHEDRAL'S PAST ALONG THE WALLS AND WINDOWS - SMALL DETAILS THAT COULD EASILY BE MISSED BUT ARE WORTH PAYING ATTENTION TO.

MEDIÆVAL PAINTINGS
Remnants of mediæval paintings that were once whitewashed can be found in the South Quire Aisle. Below the Bishop Hacket window, and on the wall behind a Saxon monument, is a large but badly-damaged mediæval wall painting representing the Holy Trinity. A small painting of the Crucifixion can be found inside an opening in the wall, thought to have been a mediæval piscina (a washbasin), indicating an altar may have been placed here. This area is thought to have been a mediæval chapel dedicated to St Nicholas, the patron saint of children.

SLEEPING CHILDREN
This former chapel now houses a monument called the 'Sleeping Children' by Sir Francis Chantrey. These two children were Ellen Jane and Marianne Robinson. Their mother, Mrs Robinson lost her husband and both children in the space of three years and in her grief commissioned a sculptor to produce this realistic and moving memorial. Mrs Robinson's father was Dean of Lichfield, and the monument came to the Cathedral in 1817 after its exhibition at the Royal Academy in London.

'And the one who was seated on the throne said, 'See, I am making all things new.' (Revelation 21.5)

DID YOU KNOW?

Bishop Hacket is one of the key figures in the history of the Cathedral. It was his herculean effort after the destruction of the Civil War that saw the Cathedral restored and functional as a place of worship again. You can see a number of tributes to him around the building:

- A stained-glass window in the South Quire Aisle shows the restoration work including scaffolding, a collapsed central spire, and Bishop Hacket himself reviewing the plans

- A monument to Bishop Hacket further down the aisle features a highly coloured effigy of him

WHAT TO LOOK FOR:

- The carved stone heads on the walls in both Quire aisles tell the story of the Cathedral's past. You can see original mediæval carvings, Victorian replacements, and some of the severely damaged heads from historic conflicts

- At the east end of the North Quire Aisle is a large stone reredos, which was originally behind the altar in St Stephen's Chapel when it was used as a chapel

- The rescuer of the Herkenrode glass, Sir Brooke Boothby, is honoured in a window at the east end of the South Quire Aisle, which incorporates some of the glass from Herkenrode

MEDIÆVAL PILGRIMAGE

The South Quire Aisle formed part of the route taken by mediæval pilgrims through the Cathedral. It is believed they gathered beneath the gallery of the St Chad's Head Chapel to wait for the gilded skull of St Chad to be displayed to them, rather than climbing the narrow staircase that leads to the Chapel.

HODSON MONUMENTS

Two monuments near the gates to the Crossing are very elaborate. They were both designed by the nineteenth century architect G. E. Street in memory of two members of the Hodson family, Archdeacon Hodson and Major Hodson.

Above: Stained glass window showing restoration of the Cathedral and collapsed central spire
Opposite (top): The Sleeping Children by Sir Francis Chantre
Opposite (middle left): Carved stone angel next to defaced angels
Opposite (middle right): Wooden lion carved into the Cathedra, Bishop's Seat
Opposite (bottom): A mediæval wall painting representing the Holy Trinity

8. LADY CHAPEL AND SHRINE OF ST CHAD

ALTHOUGH IT HAS CHANGED ITS FUNCTION AND ITS RELATIONSHIP TO THE REST OF THE CATHEDRAL OVER THE CENTURIES, THE LADY CHAPEL STILL RETAINS THE BASIC DESIGN OF THE ORIGINAL CHAPEL. HERE, BOTH PATRON SAINTS OF LICHFIELD CATHEDRAL ARE HONOURED, WITH THE CHAPEL ITSELF BEING DEDICATED TO THE BLESSED VIRGIN MARY AND THE SHRINE OF ST CHAD NOW REINSTATED IN ITS ORIGINAL POSITION.

FOUNDING FATHERS

At the entrance to the Chapel on the north side is a monument to Bishop Lonsdale, who was bishop during the nineteenth century restoration. This is flanked by carvings of Bishop Hedda, who founded the first Cathedral on this site, and Bishop de Langton, who paid for the Lady Chapel at the end of the 13th century.

DID YOU KNOW?

Most of the stained glass in the Lady Chapel was rescued from Herkenrode, a Belgian abbey in the 17th century. From 2009-2015 the glass was carefully removed (replaced with clear glass) and expertly restored by The Barley Studio, York. The plain glass was left in place to help protect the newly restored windows from the elements.

HERKENRODE WINDOWS

Through damage during the Reformation and the English Civil War, the mediæval glass had disappeared. In 1802 a local landowner, Sir Brooke Boothby, found coloured glass from the Roman Catholic abbey at Herkenrode, which had been removed during the upheavals of the French revolutionary wars. He purchased the sixteenth-century glass, and it was installed in seven of the windows here in Lichfield. The central image is that of Christ at Emmaus, and stories of the Annunciation and Holy Week are arranged in other windows.

LADY ALTAR

In the 19th century, the Kempe studio reinstated this space as a Lady Chapel. This involved the building of a 'Lady Altar', which has an English carved wooden reredos showing scenes from the Nativity (the Christmas story). The figures were made in Oberammergau, Germany, and are exquisitely decorated.

SELWYN MONUMENT

Behind the south wall of the Lady Chapel is the monument to Bishop Selwyn, who was Bishop of Lichfield from 1867 until 1878. The tiles refer to his time spent as Bishop of New Zealand and Melanesia and to a mining disaster at Pelsall colliery; Bishop Selwyn took a personal interest in the families of the dead miners. Selwyn was also the founder of Selwyn College, in Cambridge.

WHAT TO LOOK FOR:

- When repairs to the blind arcading were carried out in the nineteenth century, the masons added stone carvings of tiny angels, who can be seen praying in various positions

- At a higher level are large statues of female saints, some of whom hold the palm of martyrdom and have the instrument of their torture close by

- The canopies over the high-level Victorian statues are mediæval, and there are traces of red and green paint nearby

- The nodding ogees (14th century arches) are the most elaborate of the several forms of arcading to be found in the building and still contain a number of figures that are visible at eye level

Opposite (top): Statue of St Agnes holding a palm of martyrdom
Opposite (main): A view of the Lady Chapel from above
Below (left): Statue of the Blessed Virgin Mary and the Christ Child believed to be the work of Sir Ninian Comper
Below (right): Close up of the Selwyn Monument

'Then Mary said, "Here am I, the servant of the Lord; let it be with me according to your word."' (Luke 1.38)

SHRINE OF ST CHAD

The Lady Chapel also contains the site of the Shrine of St Chad, which was reinstated in 2022. The first shrines to contain the Saint's relics in the 7th and 8th centuries would have been elsewhere in the building, possibly the Nave. The shrine was moved to the Lady Chapel in the 13th century. Like its mediæval predecessor the shrine is for all Christians, to come and pray, and to draw strength and inspiration for their faith and life journey.

SAXON SHRINE

The first shrine was described by the Venerable Bede in 731 as being like a little wooden house. It is possible that the late eighth century Lichfield Angel formed part of the second shrine, now believed to have been housed where the Nave platform currently is.

14TH CENTURY SHRINE

In the late thirteenth century Bishop de Langton purchased a new elaborate, bejewelled shrine. A fifteenth-century eyewitness described seeing pilgrims leaving their jewels as offerings at this shrine. Lichfield was one of the foremost centres of pilgrimage in the country.

WHAT TO LOOK FOR:

- Newly-installed icons in the blind arcading depicting the life and ministry of Jesus Christ

- Two beautiful vesicas (pointed ovals) on either side of the altar; one contains the Gospel Book, the other the Blessed Sacrament for use in communion services

Above: Shrine of St Chad in the Lady Chapel
Below: Ceiling vaulting above the Retroquire and Shrine of St Chad
Opposite (left): Icon depicting The Transfiguration, written by Nicola Juha at the Bethlehem Icon Centre
Opposite (right): Reverse of the Shrine of St Chad featuring words from the Venerable Bede

DID YOU KNOW?

Who was St Chad? Born to a noble family around 634, he was educated on Lindisfarne and spent time as Bishop of York and Abbot of Lastingham. When he was appointed Bishop of Mercia, Chad chose to centre his administration in Lichfield. He founded a church and a community here in 669. Chad died in 672, much loved and revered. Bishop Hedda, his successor, consecrated the first cathedral in Lichfield on his burial site in 700.

THE REFORMATION
The Shrine remained in the Cathedral from 700 to 1538 when it was dismantled during the Reformation.

MODERN DAY SHRINE
There was no evidence left of a shrine in Lichfield Cathedral. In 1972 a commemorative floor tile was placed here to be joined later by a modern icon of St Chad by Aidan Hart. In 2022, after years of work, conversation, and growing friendship, the Shrine of St Chad was reinstated and a relic from St Chad's Cathedral, Birmingham was generously translated back to Lichfield Cathedral to be housed in the newly-built shrine altar.

The new shrine is a simple, classical altar modelled on eighth-century shrine altars. It has a silver cross under the altar surface and between the columns, given by the congregation of St Chad's Cathedral, Birmingham. The cross contains the relic. Above the altar is a crown of light (a corona) symbolising the light of Christ and the crown of glory given to his holy ones.

'A holy man, of modest character, well-read in the Scripture, and diligently practising those things which he had learned therein.' The Venerable Bede's Ecclesiastical History of the English People. (Completed around 731)

9. ST CHAD'S HEAD CHAPEL

THIS CHAPEL WAS BUILT IN THE 1220s AND WAS WHERE THE HEAD OF ST CHAD WAS KEPT IN THE MIDDLE AGES. AFTER THE REFORMATION, THE CHAPEL HAD A NUMBER OF DIFFERENT USES UNTIL IT WAS RESTORED IN THE LATE 19TH CENTURY.

DID YOU KNOW?

This work was entrusted to C. E. Kempe, who produced around twenty windows for the Cathedral and chose to fill the Chapel's original lancet windows with images of angels. They have the distinctive features of Kempe's work: coloured peacocks' feathers in their wings, rich fabrics, and delicate faces.

MUSICAL ANGELS
There are musical angels playing and singing throughout the Cathedral, recalling the story told of St Chad who was visited by angels such as these a week before his death. They play a variety of musical instruments or carry ribbons with quotations from the Psalms.

LIFE OF ST CHAD
At a high level on the west wall of the Chapel is a mediæval carving of St Chad protecting the stag that came to him for shelter, which may also show the sunbeam on which he hung his clothing. Over the door, Archbishop Theodore is shown putting the saint, who had insisted on walking through his vast Diocese, on a horse.

STONE ANGEL
On leaving the Chapel visitors often rest a hand on the head of a Victorian stone angel, which is gradually being worn away by modern pilgrims.

THE GALLERY VIEW
From the gallery there is a unique view of the Quire, the Pedilavium and the South Quire Aisle.

WHAT TO LOOK FOR:
- Depictions of the life of St Chad can be found in the stained glass and stone bosses
- Two green men can be found in the chapel

'For he will command his angels concerning you to guard you in all your ways.'
(Psalm 91.11)

Opposite: St Chad's Head Chapel
This page (top): Detail of gold ceiling boss
This page (main): Embroidery angel on chapel altar

10. ST MICHAEL'S CHAPEL AND SOUTH TRANSEPT

THIS AREA IS ONE OF REMEMBRANCE. IN ST MICHAEL'S CHAPEL THERE IS EVIDENCE OF A MEDIÆVAL ALTAR, WHICH WOULD HAVE BEEN USED FOR THE SAYING OF MASSES FOR THE SOULS OF THE DEAD. IN LATER CENTURIES MEN AND WOMEN WERE HONOURED ON WALL TABLETS AND OTHER MEMORIALS.

DID YOU KNOW?

The battle honours of the Staffordshire Regiment is summed up in the Standards (beneath the great window), which, by tradition, will hang there until they fade away.

MILITARY MEMORIALS

In 1926 the Chapel was dedicated as the Chapel of the Staffordshire Regiment, and consequently there is a cluster of military memorials. A monument topped with a sphinx commemorates the campaigns of the 80th Regiment of Foot, including its involvement in the Nile Campaign (1801-2). It is now the Chapel of the Mercian Regiment.

BOOK OF REMEMBRANCE

The names of Staffordshire men who died in the world wars of the twentieth century are recorded in two volumes. The Book of Remembrance for the First World War is usually kept open at the first page, which lists the men lost from the small village of Abbots Bromley.

STAINED GLASS

Produced in 1895 by Kempe, the Great South Window, which is such an impressive feature of this transept, shows Christ in Glory and the spread of the Church.

The Cathedral's only surviving fragments of mediæval glass can be seen in the Chapel depicting the sun and the moon, while pieces of 16th Century Herkenrode glass left over from the Lady Chapel installation were used by Kempe to create a Crucifixion scene over the altar.

The stained-glass windows at high level were produced by the Shrewsbury firm of Betton & Evans and installed between 1818 and 1819.

Above the Great South Window is a beautiful rose window which is only visible from the outside or during a behind the scenes tour.

WHAT TO LOOK FOR:

Two famous sons of Lichfield are depicted in two busts by Richard Westmacott:

- Dr Samuel Johnson, the compiler of 'A Dictionary of the English Language' (1755)
- David Garrick, the actor

In front of South Quire Aisle gates in a glass case, is the Rummer - This early 18th century goblet holds two and a half pints. It was originally used to measure the daily allowance of beer for each of the gentlemen of the choir or vicars choral.

Opposite (top): Military standards tell the history of the Staffordshire Regiment

Opposite (bottom): Union Flag in front of the Great Window

Left: The Great South Window by Kempe

Below: Bust of Dr Samuel Johnson

'No one has greater love than this, to lay down one's life for one's friends.' (John 15.13)

THE CATHEDRAL TODAY

LICHFIELD CATHEDRAL LOOKS VERY DIFFERENT TODAY FROM ITS MEDIÆVAL PREDECESSOR, BUT IN MANY WAYS THE CATHEDRAL REMAINS UNCHANGED: ACTS OF WORSHIP ARE OBSERVED DAILY, THE NAVE IS A PUBLIC SPACE USED FOR EVENTS, IT IS A PLACE FILLED WITH BEAUTY AND AWE, AND ITS FOUNDATION IS ROOTED IN THE CHRISTIAN FAITH.

As a place of awesome beauty, Lichfield Cathedral continues to inspire and encourage all who visit it as tourists, pilgrims, or worshippers. It is committed to the daily offering of worship and prayer, and to offer spiritual nourishment and welcome to all who come on their own journey of search and discovery.

In addition to daily services, the Cathedral also acts as a stunning venue for a range of events including concerts, gala dinners, festivals, awards ceremonies, performances, debates, educational forums and more.

Today, the Cathedral has four values at the centre of all that it does:

HOPE
Presenting the opportunity for people to find beauty, delight and to be uplifted.

HOSPITALITY
Providing an open door, a warm welcome and space that is open to all.

HEALING
Seeking to be a place where visitors can find a sense of wellbeing.

HOLINESS
Inspiring people to find a moment of calm, reflection, and mindfulness.

GET INVOLVED

LICHFIELD CATHEDRAL HAS A FAMILY OF STAFF, VOLUNTEERS, AND SUPPORTERS FROM ACROSS THE WORLD WHO HELP TO KEEP IT RUNNING SMOOTHLY FOR 365 DAYS PER YEAR.

JOIN THE TEAM

When there are opportunities to join the staff team they will be advertised on the website:
www.lichfield-cathedral.org/get-involved

VOLUNTEER

Take up one of the many opportunities to volunteer for Team Cathedral. You'll be joining a friendly, diverse team, gaining valuable experience as you play your part in this community.

Some of the areas for volunteering include Hospitality, Caring for the Cathedral, Creativity and Work Experience. Contact: **volunteers@lichfield-cathedral.org** to find out more.

GIVE TO LICHFIELD CATHEDRAL

It costs approximately £5,000 per day to keep Lichfield Cathedral open to visitors and as a place of worship.

There are a number of ways you can give to the Cathedral: by starting a regular gift by standing order, donating via our website, or leaving a bequest to the Cathedral.

Opposite (top): A visitor contemplates the Icon of Jesus suspended in the Nave
Opposite (below): Lichfield Cathedral Choir sing Evensong
Left: A group of visitors take a tour at the Cathedral
Above: Staff and volunteers welcome visitors to the Cathedral

CALENDAR OF EVENTS

Spring

St Chad's Day
Honouring the first Bishop of Lichfield, our co-patron

Lady Day
Mary is told she will give birth to Jesus Christ

Palm Sunday
Jesus enters Jerusalem – First day of Holy Week

Holy Week/Easter
Marking Jesus's journey from death to new life

Ascension Day
Jesus rises into Heaven

Pentecost Sunday
The Church's birthday

Summer

Corpus Christi
Thanksgiving for the tradition of Holy Communion

St James's Day
One of the twelve disciples of Jesus and the first of the Apostles to be martyred

Mary Magdalene's Day
Mary, a follower of Jesus, witnessed Jesus's death and resurrection

Transfiguration
Jesus's divinity is shown for the first time

Autumn

Holy Cross Day
Honouring Jesus's death on the cross

Michaelmas
Celebrating the work of angels

Harvest
Giving thanks for God's generosity in nature

All Saints' Day
Recalling people who have lived as examples of God's love

All Souls' Day
Giving thanks for the dearly departed

Remembrance
Remembering those who died in war and praying for peace

Advent
Waiting for the arrival of Jesus

Winter

Christmas
A time to marvel at God coming down to earth as a baby

Epiphany
The Magi follow a star to find Jesus

Candlemas
Jesus presented in the temple - marks the end of Christmas

Ash Wednesday
Lent begins: a time of contemplation

For latest information about events and Lichfield Cathedral visit: www.lichfield-cathedral.org/whatson